1-200d   19.90

I Can Read

Spanish

Compiled by

PENROSE COLYER

---

with Spanish text by

MARIA DOLORES GARCIA MOLINER

illustrated by

COLIN MIER and WENDY LEWIS

He sleeps beneath the stars.
He roams from place to place.
His name is Miguel and his adventures,
told in this book in English and in Spanish,
are sure to delight you.
You'll not only be entertained by reading them.
You'll be introduced to Spanish,
one of the most important languages in the world.

The Millbrook Press Inc.

My First English – Spanish Word Book

I Can Read
Spanish

la casa   the house

una manzana   an apple

Copyright © 1972 by Eurobook Limited
Spanish text © 1976 by Eurobook Limited
This edition © 1994 by Eurobook Limited
Published by agreement with Eurobook Limited, England

Library of Congress Cataloging-in-Publication Data
Colyer, Penrose.
  I can read Spanish: my first English-Spanish word book / by
Penrose Colyer : with Spanish text by Maria Dolores Garcia Moliner.
  p. cm.
  ISBN 1-56294-547-5   ISBN 1-56294-755-9 (p/b)
  1. Spanish language—Readers. I. Moliner, Maria. II. Title.
PC4115.C574 1994
468.6'421-dc20   94-25774
                                            CIP
                                            AC

SUMMARY: This book teaches children how to read Spanish through
simple illustrated stories in Spanish with English translations.

Printed in Italy by
Grafiche Editoriali Padane, Cremona

Contents

19.90$

Reading Spanish

Muchas gracias

Adiós

¿Cómo está usted?

You are probably already familiar with the Spanish language through widely-used words and phrases such as these, meaning "thanks", "bye", and "how are you"? Spanish is the official language of Spain and much of Latin America. People outside of Spain and Latin America also speak Spanish. The United States, for example, has almost 15 million Spanish speakers. There are about 300 million Spanish speakers worldwide.

How people speak Spanish varies somewhat from place to place. Many people in Spain speak a kind of Spanish known as Castilian. People in Latin America speak what is sometimes called American Spanish. There are other variations as well.

Whether you visit Madrid, Spain's capital, or Mexico City, or if you never set foot in a Spanish-speaking country, chances are you'll encounter this important and popular language. When you do, you may need not only to speak Spanish, but to read it as well. This book will help you practice reading Spanish.

Pronunciation

In reading Spanish, and most other languages, it helps to know how the words you're reading should sound. Spanish differs from many other languages in that it is phonetic. This means that words sound just as they are spelled. This makes Spanish easy to read and speak. There are, however some things you will need to know to read Spanish.

Vowels Five vowels make up the Spanish language. All have short sounds. They are:

a	pronounced like the *a* in father
e	pronounced like the *e* in pen
i or *y*	pronounced like the *i* in police
o	pronounced like the *o* in go
u	pronounced like the *u* in truth

Consonants Spanish has four consonants that English does not have. They are:

ch	pronounced like the *ch* in church
ll	pronounced like the *y* in yellow
ñ	pronounced like the *ny* in canyon
rr	pronounced by rolling the tongue

as if imitating a ringing telephone: *rrrring*

Other consonant sounds A few other consonant sounds may be new to you as well. They are:

h	never pronounced
j	always pronounced as *h* as in how
v	always pronounced as *b* as in boy
z, c	followed by *i* or *e*

generally pronounced in American Spanish like the *s* in sun

generally pronounced in Castilian like the *th* in thought.

Reading Tips

A few other tips may help you learn to read Spanish.

Abbreviation Most written languages use shortened forms of words, or abbreviations. You've probably seen *feet* written as *ft*. There are several abbreviations used in written Spanish. They are:

Sr. which stands for *Señor*, meaning "Mr."
Sra. which stands for *Señora*, meaning "Mrs." or "Ms."
Srta. which stands for *Señorita*, meaning "Miss." or "Ms."
Ud. which stands for *Usted*, meaning "you".
Uds. which stands for *Ustedes*, meaning "you" (plural).

Accent Spanish has one written accent, the ´. This accent can only be placed above a vowel. There are four instances in which it is used. They are:

▶ To show where the strongest syllable in a particular word is, such as *eléctrico*.

▶ To show the different meanings of words that are spelled the same, such as *él* ("he") rather than *el* ("the"); *sí* ("yes") rather than *si* ("if"); *tú* ("you") rather than *tu* ("your").

▶ Over words in questions, such as *¿dónde?* ("where?")

▶ Over words in exclamations, such as *¡Qué horror!* ("what horror!")

Capitalization Many words that begin with capital letters in English do not appear capitalized in Spanish. They are:

Days of the week: *lunes* ("Monday")

Months of the year: *agosto* ("August")

Adjectives of nationality: *italiano* ("Italian")

Form of address When you read a Spanish passage translated into English, you'll notice that *usted* and *tú* can both be translated as "you". In fact, these two terms are both ways of addressing someone. A person is addressed as *usted* or *tú*, depending on who that person is. If he or she is the speaker's friend, relative or child, the speaker says *tú*. (*Tú* is also used to address a pet.) If he or she doesn't fit into these categories, the speaker uses *usted*.

Gender Spanish nouns are classed as either masculine or feminine. Generally, masculine nouns end in the letters o, l, or r. Feminine nouns end in *a, ion,* or *d*. Because of this, you'll often (but not always) see the words *el* or *los* in front of a masculine noun and *la* or *las* in front of a feminine noun. (*Los* and *las* are the plural of *el* and *la*).

Order The order of words in Spanish sentences resembles the order found in English sentences, with some differences. In Spanish, verbs follow pronouns. Here's an example:

If you say in English: She gives us the book.

You would say in Spanish: *Ella nos da el libro.*

Which would literally mean: She to us gives the book.

Another difference in word order has to do with adjectives. In Spanish, adjectives follow the nouns they modify. Here's an example:

If you say in English: She gives us the black book.

You would say in Spanish: *Ella nos da el libro negro.*

Which would literally mean: She to us gives the book black.

Punctuation In Spanish, exclamations are punctuated at the beginning with upside-down exclamation points and at the end with regular exclamation points. Here's an example:

¡Ella nos da el libro negro!

She gives us the black book!

Questions are also punctuated at the beginning, with upside-down question marks. Something else to notice about a question in Spanish is that it begins with the sentence's main verb:

¿Da ella el libro negro a nosotros?

Did she give the black book to us?

Quotation marks are not used in written Spanish.

Instead, a dash is used to show that somebody is speaking.

Ella dice—¿Tienes el libro negro?

She says, "Do you have the black book?"

The verb to be In reading Spanish, you'll notice that both *es* and *está* mean "is". These are two forms of the two separate verbs Spanish has meaning "to be", *ser* and *estar*. These verbs can't be used interchangeably. In general, *ser* is used when talking about a state of being that can't be changed, such as nationality. Here's an example:

Yo soy americano.

I am American.

Soy is a form of *ser*, used because nationality is permanent.

Estar is generally used when talking about a state of being that can change. Here's an example:

Yo estoy cansado.

I am tired.

Estoy is a form of *estar*, used because tiredness is temporary.

You don't have to remember all of these rules to read Spanish. They're simply here to refer to if you get confused about certain points. The best way to use this book is to read the Spanish phrases and sentences and then read them in English. After a while, you'll learn what the Spanish words mean in English and you'll be on your way to saying: "I can read Spanish".

Los amigos de Miguel
Mike's friends

Miguel / Mike
Miguel es un vagabundo.
Mike is a tramp.
Es también el héroe de este libro.
He is also the hero of this book.
Aquí son algunos de sus amigos.
Here are some of his friends.

Mauricio / Maurice
Mauricio es el loro de Miguel.
Maurice is Mike's parrot.
Tiene plumas verdes.
He has green feathers.
Está muy orgulloso de sus plumas.
He is very proud of his feathers.

Alberto / Albert
Alberto es el gato de Miguel.
Albert is Mike's cat.
En verano, Alberto acompaña a Miguel.
In summer Albert stays with Mike.
Pero en invierno hace frío.
But in winter it's cold.
A Alberto no le gusta el frío.
Albert doesn't like the cold.
En invierno, Alberto va a casa de la
Sra. de Molinero.
In winter, Albert goes to Mrs. de Molinero's house.

Sra. de Molinero / Mrs. de Molinero
La Sra. de Molinero es una vieja amiga de Miguel.
Mrs. de Molinero is an old friend of Mike's.
Presta a Miguel el baño, y a veces
la cocina.
*She lends Mike her bathroom, and
sometimes, her kitchen.*

Cristóbal / Christopher
Cristóbal es hijo del Sr. Caballero.
Christopher is Mr. Caballero's son.
Cristóbal es muy delgado.
Christopher is very thin.
Es un vendedor de helados.
He is an ice-cream seller.
A veces da un helado a Miguel.
Sometimes he gives Mike an ice-cream.

Jorge / George
Jorge es el guardián del zoológico.
George is the keeper at the zoo.
Jorge a menudo da a Miguel un billete
gratis para el zoológico.
*George often gives Mike a free ticket for
the zoo.*
A Miguel le gusta mucho ir al zoológico.
Mike loves going to the zoo.

Sr. Caballero / Mr. Caballero
El Sr. Caballero es panadero.
Mr. Caballero is a baker.
Es muy gordo.
He is very fat.
Come mucho pan y tortas.
He eats a lot of bread and cakes.
A veces da tortas a Miguel.
Sometimes he gives Mike some cakes.

Srta. Colina / Miss Colina
La Srta. Colina es maestra.
Miss Colina is a teacher.
Presta libros a Miguel.
She lends Mike books.
Pero Miguel no sabe leer.
But Mike can't read.
La Srta. Colina enseña a Miguel a leer.
Miss Colina gives Mike reading lessons.

Sr. Moreno / *Mr. Moreno*

El Sr. Moreno es granjero.
Mr. Moreno is a farmer.
Tiene un granero y muchos animales.
He has a barn and a lot of animals.
En invierno, Miguel duerme en el granero.
In winter, Mike sleeps in the barn.

Profesor Julián / *Professor Julian*

Al Profesor Julián le interesan las estrellas.
Professor Julian is interested in the stars.
Las observa toda la noche.
He looks at them all night long.
Habla a Miguel de las estrellas.
He talks about the stars to Mike.

Silvia / *Sylvia*

Silvia es acomodadora en el cine.
Sylvia is an usherette at the movies.
Algunas veces da a Miguel una entrada gratuita.
Sometimes she gives Mike a free ticket.

Pedro / *Peter*

Pedro es astronauta.
Peter is an astronaut.
Habla a Miguel de la Luna.
He talks about the moon to Mike.
Miguel quiere ir a la Luna.
Mike wants to go to the moon.

Sra. de Blanco / *Mrs. de Blanco*

La Sra. de Blanco es una conductora de taxi.
Mrs. de Blanco is a taxi driver.
Algunas veces lleva a Miguel de paseo en su taxi.
Sometimes she gives Mike a ride in her taxi.

Jerónimo / *Jeremy*

Jerónimo es gitano.
Jeremy is a gypsy.
Atrapa muchos conejos.
He catches a lot of rabbits.
A menudo da un conejo a Miguel.
He often gives Mike a rabbit.

María Moreno / *Mary Moreno*

María Moreno es hija del Sr. Moreno.
Mary Moreno is Mr. Moreno's daughter.
No sabe nadar.
She can't swim.
Miguel da lecciones de natación a Maria.
Mike gives Mary swimming lessons.

Juan / *John*

A Juan le gusta mucho ir a ver partidos de fútbol.
John loves watching soccer matches.
A menudo Miguel le acompaña.
Often Mike goes with him.

Fidel / *Fido*

Fidel es el amigo fiel de Miguel.
Fido is Mike's faithful friend.
El guarda a Miguel.
He guards Mike.
Pero a menudo, cuando está de guardia, Fidel se duerme.
But often, when he is on guard, Fido falls asleep.

The last names of Mike's friends have meanings in English. They are:

> Blanco, *white*
> Caballero, *gentleman, knight*
> Colina, *hill*
> Molinero, *miller*
> Moreno, *brown*

Cristóbal Caballero
Christopher Caballero

Jorge, el guardián del zoológico
George, the keeper at the zoo

Mauricio,
el loro de Migue
*Maurice,
Mike's parrot*

Sra. de Molinero
Mrs. de Molinero

Sr. Caballero
Mr. Caballero

Fidel, el perro
Fido, the dog

Srta. Colina
Miss Colina

Juan
John

e Miguel   Mike's friends

Pedro
Peter

Jerónimo, el gitano
Jeremy, the gypsy

Profesor Julián
Professor Julian

r. Moreno
Ir. Moreno

Sra. de Blanco
Mrs. de Blanco

Silvia
Sylvia

María Moreno
Mary Moreno

Alberto, el gato
Albert, the cat

¿Cuántos?
How many?

Cuatro botellas de Coca-Cola
Four bottles of Coca-Cola

¿Te gusta la Coca-Cola?
Do you like Coca-Cola?

Dos grandes dragones
Two large dragons

Una isla
One island

¿Cuántas personas hay en la isla?
How many people are there on the island?

Seis paraguas
Six umbrellas

¿Cuántas gotas de lluvia hay?
How many raindrops are there?

Tres girafas
Three giraffes

¿Cuántos ojos tienen?
How many eyes do they have?

¿Y cuántas manchas?
And how many spots?

¿Cien?
A hundred?

12

¿Cuántas?
How many?

Velas
Candles

Es el cumpleaños de alguien.
It's somebody's birthday.

Cumple nueve años.
He is nine.

Diez carpas doradas
Ten goldfish

Cinco herraduras de buena suerte
Five lucky horseshoes

¿Tiene suerte este hombre?
Is this man lucky?

Cepillos de dientes de una familia numerosa
The toothbrushes of a large family
En la familia hay ocho niños.
There are eight children in the family.

Aquí hay siete hombres.
Here are seven men.

 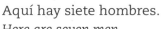

Hay tres vaqueros y cuatro pistoleros.
There are three cowboys and four gangsters.

¿Quién está ganando?
Who is winning?

13

En el zoológico
At the zoo

Dos girafas
Two giraffes
Una girafa se llama Genoveva.
One giraffe is called Genevieve.
El otro se llama Alfonso.
The other one is called Alphonse.

Un tigre
A tiger

Mauricio habla
con los loros.
*Maurice is talking
to the parrots.*

Gorilas
Gorillas

Un hipopótamo
A hippopotamus

Un oso
A bear

Un águila
An eagle
Odia a los visitantes.
He hates visitors.

Jorge, el guardián
George, the keeper
Habla con los monos.
He is talking to the monkeys.
Los entiende muy bien.
He understands them very well.

14

Un león y una leona
A lion and a lioness
Tienen hambre.
They are hungry.

Focas
Seals
Les gusta mucho zambullirse.
They love diving.

Un elefante
An elephant

Una serpiente
A snake

Un cocodrilo
A crocodile

La trompa del elefante
The elephant's trunk

Un flamenco
A flamingo

El Sr. Caballero da bizcochos a los pingüinos.
Mr. Caballero is giving the penguins some cakes.

15

Jorge y Genoveva
George and Genevieve

Jorge es un guardián del zoológico.
George is a keeper at the zoo.
Está muy preocupado.
He is very worried.

La girafa Genoveva no quiere comer.
Genevieve the giraffe refuses to eat.
Está adelgazando.
She is getting thin.

Jorge da heno a Genoveva.
George gives Genevieve some hay.
Pero ella no quiere comerlo.
But she refuses to eat it.

Jorge da hojas verdes a Genoveva.
George gives Genevieve some green leaves.
Pero ella no quiere comerlas.
But she refuses to eat them.
Está más y más delgada.
She is getting thinner and thinner.

Genoveva está muy, muy delgada.
Geneviève is very, very thin.
El jefe del zoológico va a verla.
The head of the zoo goes to see her.

¡Anda, come!—dice el jefe a Genoveva.
"Go on, eat!" says the head to Genevieve.
Pero ella no quiere comer.
But she refuses to eat.

¡Genoveva es libre!
Geneviève is free!

Tiene mucha hambre.
She is very, very hungry.

Come las hojas de los árboles del zoológico.
She eats the leaves of the trees in the zoo.

Jorge está desesperado.
George is in despair.
Genoveva se va a morir.
Geneviève is going to die.

Pero Genoveva no se muere.
But Geneviève does not die.
Por la noche se escapa entre las barras de su jaula.
At night, she slips between the bars of her cage.

Genoveva se escapa.
Geneviève escapes.
¡Adiós, zoológico!
Good-bye zoo!

Genoveva se siente muy feliz.
Geneviève is very happy.
Pero Jorge y el jefe del zoológico están furiosos.
But George and the head of the zoo are furious.

Miguel toma un baño

A Miguel le gusta mucho tomar un baño.
Mike loves taking a bath.

Los dedos de los pies de Miguel
Mike's toes
¿Cuántos dedos tiene en los pies?
How many toes does he have?

Una bañera roja
A red bathtub

Miguel se ha lavado hasta aquí.
Mike has washed up to here.

Jabón
Soap

Un cepillo largo
A long brush

Alberto ha pasado por aquí.
Albert has walked here.
A Alberto no le gusta lavarse.
Albert does not like washing.

¿Quién ha pasado por aquí?
Who has walked here?

Mike takes a bath

Una ventana
A window

A Mauricio no le gusta lavarse.
Maurice doesn't like washing.
Le tiene miedo al agua.
He's frightened of water.

Una maceta de flores
A flower pot
La flor está muerta.
The flower is dead.

Dentífrico
Toothpaste

Un cepillo de dientes
A toothbrush

Un vaso
A glass

Dentadura postiza
False teeth

Gotas de agua
Drops of water

Mauricio ha pasado por aquí.
Maurice has walked here.

Un pato de plástico
A plastic duck

Quieren ser . . .
They want to be . . .

La Sra. de Molinero quiere ser bailarina
de ballet.
Mrs. de Molinero wants to be a ballet dancer.

El Sr. Caballero quiere más que nada ser delgado
Mr. Caballero wants most of all to be thin.
Luego quiere ser vaquero.
Then he wants to be a cowboy.

Fidel quiere ser un perro de lanas.
Fido wants to be a poodle.
Quiere ganar premios en competiciones.
He wants to win prizes in competitions.

La Srta. Colina quiere ser espía.
Miss Colina wants to be a spy.
Quiere ser bella y peligrosa.
She wants to be beautiful and dangerous.

Jerónimo quiere ser pirata.
Jeremy wants to be a pirate.
Quiere ir en barco a países lejanos.
He wants to go in a ship to far-off countries.

Jorge quiere ser pintor.
George wants to be a painter.
Quiere pintar retratos de todos los animales
del zoológico.
*He wants to paint portraits of all the
animals in the zoo.*

María Moreno quiere ser cantante de "pop".
Mary Moreno wants to be a pop singer.

Pedro ya se ha cansado de la Luna y las estrellas.
Peter has had enough of the moon and the stars.
Quiere explorar el fondo del mar.
He wants to be an underwater explorer.

El Profesor Julián quiere ser astronauta.
Professor Julian wants to be an astronaut.
Quiere estar más cerca de las estrellas.
He wants to be closer to the stars.

Juan quiere ser jugador profesional de fútbol.
John wants to be a professional soccer player.
O locutor.
Or an announcer.

Al Sr. Moreno le gusta el dinero.
Mr. Moreno likes money.
Quiere ser millonario.
He wants to be a millionaire.

La Sra. de Blanco ya se ha cansado de
conducir pasajeros.
*Mrs. de Blanco has had enough of driving
people in her taxi.*
Quiere ser rica.
She wants to be rich.
Y viajar de pasajera en los taxis.
She wants to take taxis herself.

El Sr. Caballero en la cocina
Mr. Caballero in the kitchen

La gata del Sr. Caballero
Mr. Caballero's cat
Es muy gorda y muy perezosa.
She is very fat and very lazy.

Tortas
Cakes
Al Sr. Caballero le gustan
mucho las tortas.
Mr. Caballero loves cakes.

Una cocina
A stove

Un fregadero
A sink

Un lavaplatos
A dishwasher
A la Sra. de Caballero no le gusta lavar platos.
Mrs. de Caballero doesn't like washing dishes.

Un horno
An oven

Una batidora eléctrica
An electric mixer

Ratones
Mice

Libros de recetas de cocina
Recipe books

¿Cuantos libros hay allí?
How many books are there?

Una mesa
A table

Una estrella
A star

La Luna
The moon

Un reloj
de cuclillo
A cuckoo
clock

Es medianoche.
It's midnight.

El Sr. Caballero viste pijama.
Mr. Caballero is in his pajamas.
Tiene hambre.
He is hungry.

Un vaso de leche
A glass of milk

Una nevera
A refrigerator

Queso
Cheese

Huevos
Eggs

Fruta
Fruit

¿Dónde viven?
Where do they live?

El bebé vive en su cuna.
The baby lives in a crib.
El odia su cuna.
He hates his crib.

Los marcianos viven en Marte.
The Martians live on Mars.

La abuela vive en un chalet.
Granny lives in a bungalow.

El oso vive en las montañas.
The bear lives in the mountains.

Los gemelos viven en un rascacielos.
The twins live in a skyscraper.
Su piso es el treintavo.
They are on the thirtieth floor.

Jorge tiene su casa en un árbol.
George lives in a tree-house.
No es muy sólida.
It's not very strong.

Los ratones viven en un agujero.
The mice live in a hole.
Es muy oscuro.
It's very dark.

En invierno, Miguel vive debajo de un puente.
In winter, Mike lives under a bridge.

Los astronautas quieren vivir en la Luna.
The astronauts want to live on the moon.

En verano, Miguel vive debajo de un árbol.
In summer, Mike lives under a tree.

El marinero vive en un barco.
The sailor lives on a ship.
Algunas veces se marea.
Sometimes he is seasick.

El Rey vive en su castillo.
The King lives in his castle.
Hace un poco de frío allí.
It's a bit cold there.

El pastor vive en una choza, con el rebaño.
The shepherd lives in a hut, with the lambs.

El mono vive en las selva.
The monkey lives in the jungle.

El gitano vive en una casa rodante.
The gypsy lives in a wagon.

El helicóptero
The helicopter

El piloto
The pilot
Está cantando.
He is singing.
Le gusta mucho volar.
He loves flying.

El pasajero
The passenger
Se siente mareado.
He is feeling airsick.
Quiere aterrizar.
He wants to land.

Rebaños de borregos
Sheep

Una fábrica
A factory

Chimeneas
Chimneys

Un puente
A bridge

Un río
A river

Un camión
A truck

Un caballo
A horse

Un tren
A train

Si yo fuera millonario . . .

If I were a millionaire . . .

Daría la vuelta al mundo.
I would go around the world.

Compraría una isla.
I would buy an island.

Me compraría un tren y lo conduciría.
I would buy a train and drive it.

Comería doce helados todos los días.
I would eat twelve ice-creams every day.

Viviría en una selva con mis amigos.
I would live in a forest with my friends.

Tendría una casa debajo del mar.
I would have a house under the sea.

Iría a la Luna.
I would go to the moon.

Iría al circo todos los días.
I would go to the circus every day.

Me compraría mil globos y volaría.
I would buy a thousand balloons and I would fly.

Viviría en una casa rodante . . .
I would live in a wagon . . .

. . . O tal vez en una moderna casa rodante.
. . . Or perhaps in a modern trailer.

La natación Swimming

A Miguel la natación le parece fatigosa.
Mike finds swimming exhausting.

A Miguel le gustan mucho los helados de fresa.
Mike loves strawberry ice-cream.

El rojo y el naranja son los colores favoritos de Miguel
Red and orange are Mike's favourite colors.

Un helado
An ice-cream

A Miguel le gusta mucho cocina
Mike loves cooking.
La cocina de Miguel
Mike's kitchen

Un flotador
Water wings

Un bañador
Bathing trunks

Un pez
A fish
El pez se está comiendo el flotador.
The fish is eating the water wings.

El sol
The sun

Un helicóptero
A helicopter

Un árbol
A tree

Una vaca
A cow
Está comiendo los calzoncillos de Miguel.
She is eating Mike's pants.

Los calzoncillos de Miguel
Mike's pants

Fidel, el perro de Miguel
Mike's dog Fido
Guarda la ropa de Miguel.
He is guarding Mike's clothes.

El sombrero de Miguel
Mike's hat

La camisa de Miguel
Mike's shirt

Un pato
A duck

Una libélula
A dragon-fly
Está observando a Miguel.
It is watching Mike.

Una rana
A frog
Está observando la libélula.
It is watching the dragon-fly.

31

Miguel mira la televisión
Mike looks at television

Miguel no tiene televisor.
Mike doesn't have television.
Pero le gusta mucho mirar la televisión
But he loves watching television.

Miguel va a la ciudad.
Mike goes into town.
Encuentra un televisor.
He finds a television set.

Mira una película de vaqueros.
He watches a western.

Imita a los cantantes.
He imitates the singers.

Después mira un programa de "pop".
Then he watches a pop program.

También imita a los comediantes . . .
He also imitates the comedians . . .

y imita a los directores de orquesta . . .
and he imitates the conductors . . .

y imita a los cocineros . . .
and he imitates the cooks . . .

y imita a los deportistas . . .
and he imitates the sportsmen . . .

y imita a los bailarines.
and he imitates the dancers.

A Miguel le gusta mucho mirar la televisión.
Mike loves watching television.
¡Y a la gente le gusta mirar a Miguel!
And people love watching Mike!

Cuadros
Paintings
¿Qué cuadro es el mejor?
Which painting is the best?

Un inglés comiendo pescado y patatas fritas.
An Englishman eating fish and chips.

Un mapa
A map

Flores
Flowers

Piedras
Stones

La piedra verde de María
Mary's green stone
Ella dice que es una piedra preciosa.
She says it is a precious stone.

Libros
Books
¿Cuántos libros puedes ver en la clase?
How many books can you see in the classroom?

El ratón de María no le gusta la televisión.
Mary's mouse doesn't like television.

Un cuaderno de ejercicios
A notebook

Una goma de borrar
An eraser

Un bolígrafo
A ballpoint

Una regla
A ruler

Un lápiz
A pencil

Chicle
Chewing gum

María Moreno en la escuela
Mary Moreno at school

La Srta. Colina
Miss Colina
Es una maestra.
She is a teacher.

A María Moreno le gustan las lecciones de inglés.
Mary Moreno likes English lessons.
Le gusta mirar la televisión.
She likes watching television.

Anna tiene miedo a los ratones.
Anna is afraid of mice.
Ella va a gritar.
She is going to scream.

Insectos
Insects

A Juan le gusta la televisión, pero solamente cuando hay fútbol.
John likes television, but only when there is soccer on.
Está leyendo una revista de fútbol.
He is reading a soccer magazine.

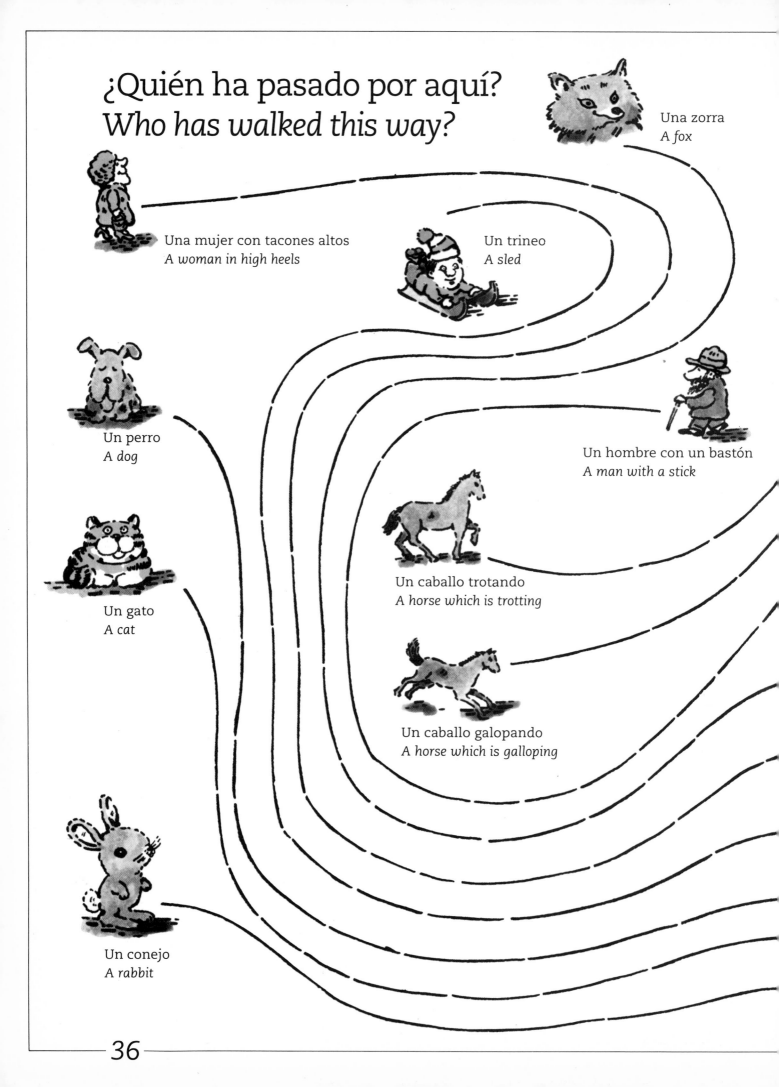

¿Quién ha pasado por aquí?
Who has walked this way?

Una zorra
A fox

Una mujer con tacones altos
A woman in high heels

Un trineo
A sled

Un perro
A dog

Un hombre con un bastón
A man with a stick

Un gato
A cat

Un caballo trotando
A horse which is trotting

Un caballo galopando
A horse which is galloping

Un conejo
A rabbit

36

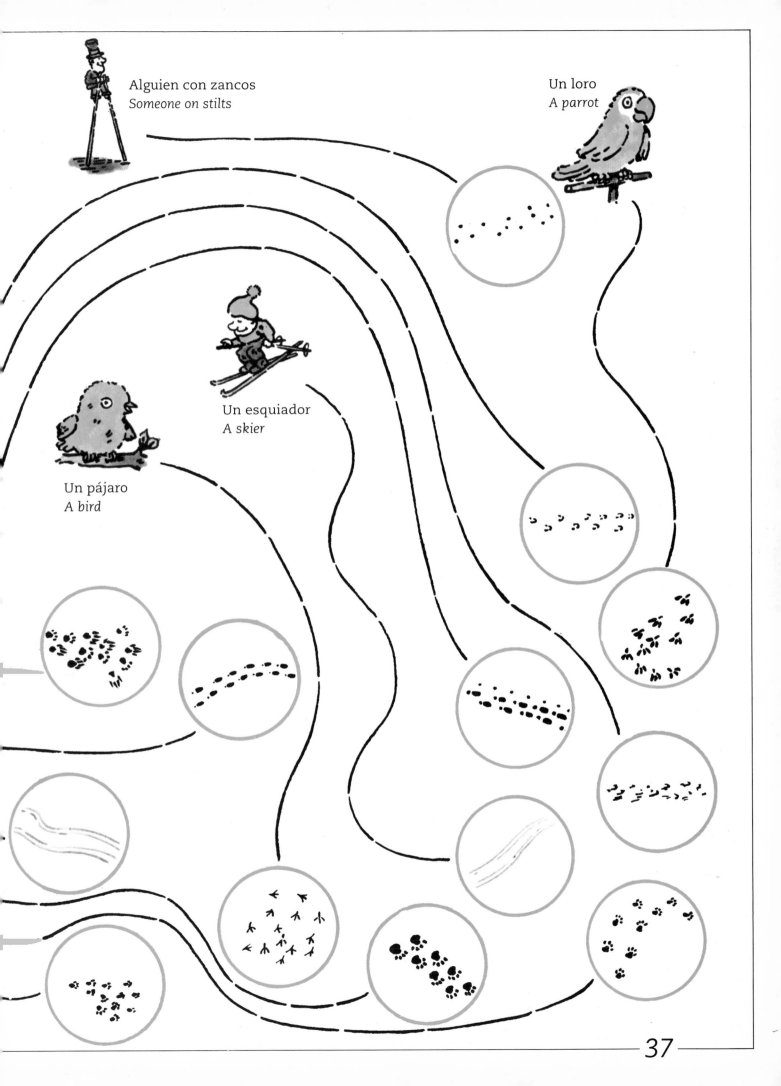

Alguien con zancos
Someone on stilts

Un loro
A parrot

Un esquiador
A skier

Un pájaro
A bird

Jerónimo el gitano se acuesta

Jerónimo está en su casa rodante.
Jeremy is in his wagon.
Afuera hace frío.
Outside it is cold.
Jerónimo está caliente.
Jeremy is warm.

El abrigo de Jerónimo está roto.
Jeremy's coat is torn.
Lo está remendando.
He is mending it.

Un despertador
An alarm clock
No funciona, pero a Jerónimo le gust[a]
It doesn't work, but Jeremy likes it.

El pijama de Jerónimo
Jeremy's pajamas

La cama de
Jerónimo
Jeremy's bed

El perro de Jerónimo
Jeremy's dog
Se llama Malvado.
He's called Wicked.
Está mirando el bocadillo.
He is looking at the sandwich.

Un bocadillo de pollo
A chicken sandwich

Jeremy the gypsy goes to bed

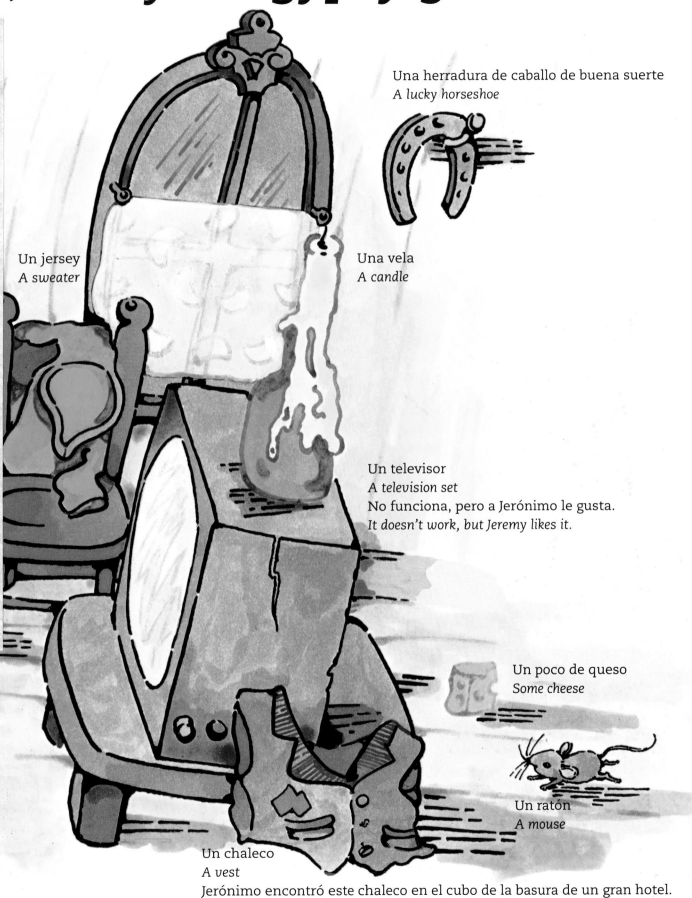

Una herradura de caballo de buena suerte
A lucky horseshoe

Un jersey
A sweater

Una vela
A candle

Un televisor
A television set
No funciona, pero a Jerónimo le gusta.
It doesn't work, but Jeremy likes it.

Un poco de queso
Some cheese

Un ratón
A mouse

Un chaleco
A vest
Jerónimo encontró este chaleco en el cubo de la basura de un gran hotel.
Jeremy found this vest in the trash can of a big hotel.

El pastel de la Sra. de Molinero
Mrs. de Molinero's cake

La Sra. de Molinero está en su cocina.
Mrs. de Molinero is in her kitchen.
Está haciendo un pastel con huevos, harina,
mantequilla y leche.
She is making a cake with eggs,
flour, butter and milk.

La Sra. de Molinero pone el pastel en el horno.
Mrs. de Molinero puts the cake in the oven.
Alberto lo observa.
Albert looks at it.

Cuando el pastel está cocido la Sra. de
Molinero lo cubre de cerezas.
When the cake is cooked, Mrs. de Molinero
puts some cherries on it.

La Sra. de Molinero sale de la cocina.
Mrs de Molinero goes out of the kitchen.
El loro Mauricio entra.
Maurice the parrot comes in.
Se come las cerezas se va volando.
He eats the cherries and flies away.

La Sra. de Molinero vuelve a la cocina.
Mrs. de Molinero comes back to the kitchen.
¡Qué horror!
How terrible!
¿Quién se ha comido las cerezas?
Who has eaten the cherries?
Debe de haber sido Alberto.
It must be Albert.

La Sra. de Molinero cubre el pastel con chocolate.
Mrs. de Molinero covers the cake with the chocolate.
Pone una cereza en el centro.
She puts one cherry in the middle.
Echa a Alberto de la cocina.
She takes Albert out of the kitchen.

Mauricio se come la cereza.
Maurice eats the cherry.

La Sra. de Molinero vuelve a la cocina.
Mrs. de Molinero comes back.
Y en el pastel ve la marca de la pata de Mauricio.
On the cake she sees a mark: Maurice's claw.

La Sra. de Molinero coje una sartén.
Mrs. de Molinero takes a saucepan.
Y se va en busca de Mauricio . . .
She is going to look for Maurice . . .

Una mariposa
A butterfly

Un árbol
A tree

Algunos gnomos
Some gnomes
¿Son reales?
Are they real?

Hojas
Leaves

Un columpio
A swing

Césped
A lawn

Un to
A mo
Está dormid
It is aslee

Una carpa dorada
A goldfish
Está dormida.
It is asleep.

Rosas
Roses

Una topinera
A mole hill

Rocío
Dew

El sol se levanta.
The sun is rising.

Un borde de arbustos
A hedge

Un ratón de campo
A field mouse
¿Cuántas crias tiene?
How many babies are there?

Un pájaro
A bird
Está tomando su baño matinal.
He is taking his morning bath.

Narcisos
Daffodils

Tulipanes
Tulips

Una oruga
A caterpillar
¿Cuántas orugas puedes ver?
How many caterpillars can you see?

Una ardilla
A squirrel
Va a buscar nueces.
He is going to find some nuts.

Regalos
Presents

Una conejilla de Indias
A guinea pig

Un traje de astronauta
An astronaut suit

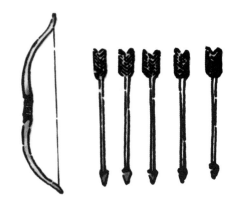

Arco y flechas
A bow and arrows

Un bote de pintura
A can of paint

Una máquina fotográfica
A camera
¿Quién está en la foto?
Who is in the photo?

Libros
Books

Cartas
Cards

Semillas de flores
Flower seeds

Una alcancía y dinero
A bank and some money

Máscaras
Masks

Un cepillo para rascarse la espalda
A back-scratcher

Un títere
A puppet

Una cometa
A kite

Un perrito
A puppy
Ponle un nombre.
Give him a name.

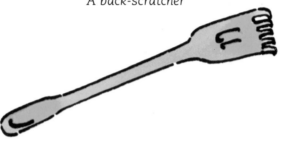

Una canoa
A canoe

Un trampolín
A trampoline

Una bicicleta
A bicycle

Azúcar
Sugar

Cacao
Cocoa

Chocolate líquido
Liquid chocolate

Nueces
Nuts

Un delantal
An apron

Caramelos
Caramels

Bombones de naranja
Orange creams

Bombones de café
Coffee creams

Alumnos y alumnas
Schoolboys and schoolgirls
¿Reconoces a alguien?
Whom do you recognize?

En la fábrica de chocolate
In the chocolate factory

Cade clase de bombones
lleva una decoración distinta.
*Each kind of chocolate
has a different decoration.*

La máquina de decorar
The decorating machine

Un pañuelo de cabeza
A scarf
Todos las empleadas
tienen que llevar un pañuelo
en la cabeza.
*All the operators
have to wear a scarf.*

Esta empleada quita
los bombones defectuosos.
*This operator takes away
faulty chocolates.*

La inspectora
The checker

ıa empleada
ı operator

Un bombón defectuoso
A faulty chocolate
¿Por qué es defectuoso?
Why is it faulty?

La encargada
The supervisor

Miguel y Juan van a un partido de fútbol
Mike and John go to a soccer match

Miguel y Juan les gusta mucho el fútbol.
Mike and John love soccer.
Van a un partido juntos.
They are going to a match together.

Los *Leones* juegan contra los *Perros Negros*.
The Lions are playing the Black Dogs.
Los dos equipos son muy fuertes.
Both teams are very strong.

En el estadio hay una gran multitud.
In the stadium there is an enormous crowd.

Miguel y Juan gritan para animar a los *Perros Negros*.
Mike and John shout to encourage the Black Dogs.

El partido comienza.
The match begins.
Los *Perros Negros* corren muy de prisa.
The Black Dogs run very fast.

El capitán de los *Perros Negros* va a meter un gol.
The captain of the Black Dogs is going to score a goal.

¡Es un gol!
It's a goal!
Pero el balón no se para.
But the ball does not stop.
¡Aterriza en la cabeza de Miguel!
It lands on Mike's head!

Miguel se queda atontado.
Mike is dazed.

Miguel y Juan van a la salida.
Mike and John go to the exit.
Llega el gerente del estadio.
The manager of the stadium arrives.

Y da entradas gratuitas a Miguel y a Juan
para el gran partido de la semana próxima.
He gives Mike and John free tickets for the big match next week.
¡Miguel y Juan están muy contentos!
Mike and John are very pleased!

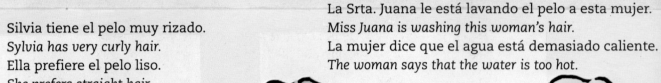

Silvia tiene el pelo muy rizado.
Sylvia has very curly hair.
Ella prefiere el pelo liso.
She prefers straight hair.

La Srta. Juana le está lavando el pelo a esta mujer.
Miss Juana is washing this woman's hair.
La mujer dice que el agua está demasiado caliente.
The woman says that the water is too hot.

A la Srta. Colina no le gusta su pelo.
Miss Colina doesn't like her hair.
Quiere cambiárselo.
She wants to change it.
Está eligiendo una peluca.
She is choosing a wig.

Barniz de uñas
Nail polish

Un peine
A comb

Una redecilla
A hair net

At the hairdresser's

La Sra. de Molinero está debajo de secador.
Mrs. de Molinero is under the dryer.
Está leyendo revistas.
She is reading magazines.

¡Qué horror!
How terrible!
¡El pelo de la Sra. de Molinero se ha vuelto verde!
Mrs de Molinero's hair has turned green!

La Srta. Anna le arregla las manos a esta mujer.
Miss Anna is giving this woman a manicure.

Un cepillo del pelo
A hairbrush

Laca
Lacquer

Bigudís
Rollers

51

De vacaciones
On vacation

En la playa
At the seashore
Busca una pala, un cubo y cinco conchas.
Find a shovel, a bucket and five shells.

Sobre un canal
On a canal
¿Te gustaría vivir en una barca?
Would you like to live on a barge?

En la montaña en invierno
In the mountains in winter
¿Quién está esquiando?
Who is skiing?
¿Sabes esquiar?
Do you know how to ski?

En el campo
In the country
¿Te gusta merendar en el campo?
Do you like picnics?
¿Qué tal tiempo hace?
What is the weather like?

En las montañas en verano
In the mountains in summer
El sol brilla pero todavía hay nieve.
The sun is shining but there is still some snow.

En una isla desierta
On a desert island
¿Hay casas en la isla?
Are there any houses on the island?

En la selva
In the jungle
Está lloviendo.
It's raining.
Los loros se ponen debajo de los árboles.
The parrots go under the trees.

En un lago
On a lake
¿Es verano o invierno?
Is it winter or summer?

El partido de hockey

Las chicas han metido cuatro gols.
The girls have scored four goals.
Los chicos han metido sólo uno.
The boys have scored only one.
Los espectadores
The spectators

Todos están gritando,—¡Bravo!
They are all shouting, "Hooray!"
Los chicos gritan menos fuerte que las chicas.
The boys are shouting less loudly than the girls.

Limones para el descanso
Lemons for half time

El árbitro
The referee
Ha corrido mucho.
He has been running a lot.
¿De qué color tiene la cara?
What color is his face?

Pantalones
cortos
Shorts

La capitana del equipo de las chicas
The captain of the girls' team
Está muy contenta.
She is very pleased.

The field hockey match

La pelota se ha ido muy lejos.
The ball has gone a long way away.
Fidel quiere encontrar la pelota.
Fido wants to find the ball.

La maestra de deportes de la escuela de
niñas está muy contenta.
*The sports teacher of the girls' school
is very pleased.*

Está muy orgullosa de su equipo.
She is very proud of the team.

¿Es niña o niño?
Is this a girl or boy?
¿Cómo lo sabes?
How do you know?

Un palo de hockey
A hockey stick

Una camisa de deporte
A sports shirt

El capitán del equipo de los niños
The captain of the boys' team
Está furioso.
He is furious.
Pretende estar contento.
He is pretending to be pleased.

En el hospital
In the hospital

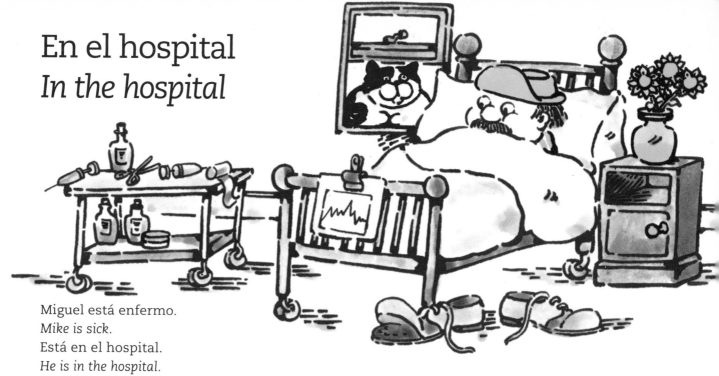

Miguel está enfermo.
Mike is sick.
Está en el hospital.
He is in the hospital.

La Sra. de Molinero visita a Miguel.
Mrs. de Molinero visits Mike.
La lleva unas flores.
She brings him some flowers.

Jorge da a Miguel un libro de billetes
para el zoológico.
*George gives Mike a book of tickets
for the zoo.*
A Miguel le gusta mucho ir al zoológico.
Mike loves going to the zoo.

El gitano Jerónimo llega.
Jeremy the gypsy arrives.
Él lleva sopa de pollo.
He brings some chicken soup.
¡Es deliciosa!
It's delicious!

El Sr. Caballero trae una gran caja.
Mr. Caballero brings a huge box.
En la caja hay seis bizcochos.
In the box there are six cakes.

Llega la Srta. Colina.
Miss Colina arrives.
Le lleva libros.
She brings some books.
Pero Miguel no sabe leer.
But Mike can't read.

Silvia da a Miguel una revista de cine.
Sylvia gives Mike a movie magazine.
En la revista hay fotografías de artistas de cine.
In the magazine there are photos of movie stars.

Cristóbal Caballero le ofrece un helado.
Christopher Caballero brings an ice cream.
Miguel tiene que comer el helado muy de prisa.
Mike has to eat the ice-cream very quickly.

Miguel está rodeado de regalos.
Mike is surrounded by presents.
Ya no se siente enfermo.
He doesn't feel sick any more.

La Sra. de Blanco llega en su taxi.
Mrs. de Blanco arrives in her taxi.
No le da ningún regalo.
She doesn't bring any presents.
¡Y se lleva a Miguel!
She takes Mike away!

En el patio de recreo
In the playground

A este niño no le gusta jugar.
This boy doesn't like to play.
Prefiere leer.
He prefers to read.
Está leyendo una revista deportiva.
He is reading a sports magazine.

Tres niñas están jugando al tres en raya.
Three girls are playing hop scotch.

Esta niña tiene una cuerda de saltar nueva.
This girl has got a new jump rope.
Puede dar trescientos saltos sin pararse.
She can do three hundred skips without stopping.

Esta niña está haciendo sus deberes.
This girl is doing her homework.

María Moreno se pone los patines.
Mary Moreno is putting on her roller skates.

Estas niñas están jugando al escondite.
These girls are playing hide and seek.
Busca a la niña que está escondida.
Find the girl who is hiding.

El niño esta fumando un cigarrillo.
The boy is smoking a cigarette.
¿De qué color tiene la cara?
What color is his face?

Juan juega al fútbol con sus amigos.
John is playing soccer with his pals.

Estos dos niños tienen hambre.
These two boys are hungry.
¿Qué están comiendo?
What are they eating?

Padres y hijos
Parents and children

Cristóbal Caballero es delgado.
Christopher Caballero is thin.
Su padre, el Sr. Caballero, es gordo.
His father, Mr. Caballero is fat.
Su madre, la Sra. de Caballero, no es ni gorda ni delgada.
His mother, Mrs. de Caballero is neither fat nor thin.

Aquí hay cuatro gusanos: abuelo, padre, hijo y nieto.
Here are four worms: grandfather, father, son and grandson.
¿Cuál es el padre?
Which is the father?

Este gigante es muy alto.
This giant is very tall.
Su hija es muy baja.
His daughter is very short.
Es una niñita.
She is a baby.

60

Este canguro lleva su hijo en su bolsa.
This kangaroo has its child in its pouch.

Este cordero no tiene madre.
This lamb has no mother.
El pastor le da leche.
The Shepherd gives it some milk.

La madre de este cachorro es una perra de lanas.
This puppy's mother is a poodle.
Su padre es un boxer.
His father is a boxer.
El cachorro no es ni perro de lanas ni boxer.
The puppy is neither a poodle nor a boxer.

He aquí un hombre, su mujer, su hijo, su hija y su perro.
Here are a man, his wife, his son, his daughter and his dog.
Se parecen el uno al otro.
They look like one another.

Pedro va a la Luna
Peter goes to the moon

Una foto de la novia de Pedro
A photo of Peter's girl friend

Una foto de los padres de Pedro
A photo of Peter's father and mother

Una foto del inventor de la nave espacial
A photo of the inventor of the spacecraft

La merienda de Pedro
Peter's tea

La comida de Pedro
Peter's lunch

El desayuno de Pedro
Peter's breakfast

El cielo es azul oscuro.
The sky is dark blue.

Estrellas
Stars

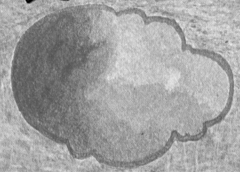

El Profesor Julián observa la nave espacial con su telescopio.
Professor Julian is looking at the spacecraft through his telescope.
A él le gustaría ir a la Luna.
He would love to go to the moon.

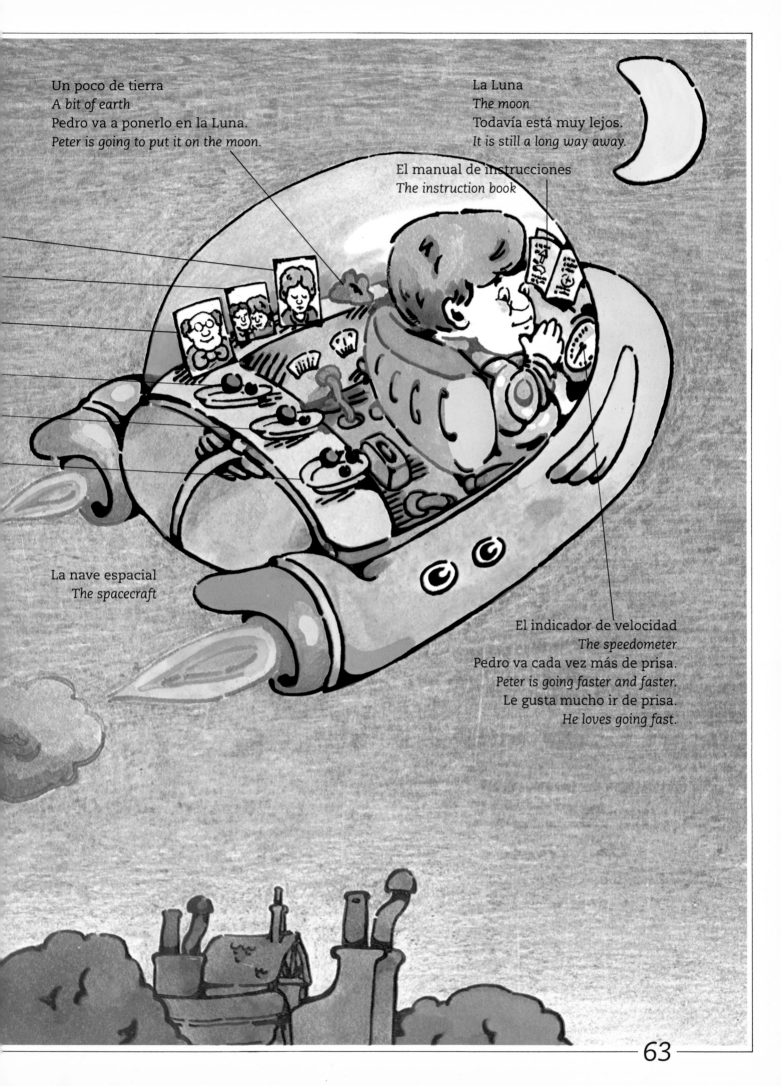

Un poco de tierra
A bit of earth
Pedro va a ponerlo en la Luna.
Peter is going to put it on the moon.

La Luna
The moon
Todavía está muy lejos.
It is still a long way away.

El manual de instrucciones
The instruction book

La nave espacial
The spacecraft

El indicador de velocidad
The speedometer
Pedro va cada vez más de prisa.
Peter is going faster and faster.
Le gusta mucho ir de prisa.
He loves going fast.

Esqueletos
Skeletons

Encuentra el dibujo que va con cada esqueleto.
Find the drawing which goes with each skeleton.

Un dinosaurio
A dinosaur
Ya no hay dinosaurios.
There are no more dinosaurs.

Un gorila
A gorilla
Su esqueleto se parece al esqueleto siguiente.
Its skeleton looks like the next skeleton.

Un hombre
A man
¿Cuántos huesos puedes ver?
How many bones can you see?

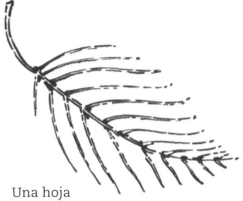

Una hoja
A leaf
Estas son nervaduras de una hoja.
Here are the veins of a leaf.

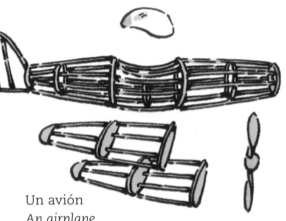

Un avión
An airplane
Este es un modelo.
This is a model.

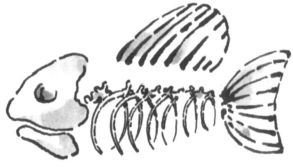

Un pez
A fish
Yo creo que es un arenque.
·I think it is a herring.

En la pista de hielo

El tenderete de los refrescos
The snack bar

Miguel intenta ponerse unos patines.
Mike is trying to put on some skates.
No quiere patinar.
He doesn't want to skate.
Tiene miedo de caerse.
He is afraid of falling down.

A Alberto le gusta mirar a los patinadores.
Albert likes watching the skaters.

El Sr. Caballero es demasiado gordo para patinar.
Mr. Caballero is too fat to skate.
Patina porque quiere adelgazar.
He skates because he wants to get thin.

Botas blancas
White boots

Silvia patina muy mal.
Sylvia skates very badly.
Pero tiene muchos amigos.
But she has a lot of friends.
Ellos la ayudan.
They help her.

Srta. Colina no patina muy bien.
Miss Colina doesn't skate very well.
Está tratando de aprender de un libro.
She is trying to learn from a book.

At the ice rink

El Sr. Moreno está mirando a Maria.
Mr. Moreno is watching Mary.
Está muy orgulloso de ella.
He is very proud of her.

Una falda corta
A short skirt

Esta señora es rusa.
This lady is Russian.
Aprendió a patinar
cuando tenía
dos años.
*She learned to skate
when she was
two years old.*

María Moreno patina muy bien.
Mary Moreno skates very well.
Ella puede bailar.
She can dance.
Es difícil seguirla con la vista.
It is difficult to watch Mary.

El profesor de patín
The skating teacher
Es muy vanidoso.
He is very conceited.

Patines
Skates

Me gusta comer . . .
I like eating . . .

Me gusta comer legumbres.
I like eating vegetables.

Me gustan particularmente:
I particularly like:

Guisantes
Peas

Zanahorias
Carrots

Patatas (especialmente fritas)
Potatoes (especially French fries)

Lechuga
Lettuce

Pepinos
Cucumbers

Coles de Bruselas
Brussels sprouts

Pero no me gustan:
But I don't like:

Espinacas
Spinach

Cebollas
Onions

68

Me gusta comer fruta.
I like eating fruit.

Mis frutas favoritas son:
My favorite fruits are:

Piñas
Pineapples

Peras
Pears

Pomelos (y jugo de pomelos)
Grapefruit (and grapefruit juice)

Guineos
Bananas

Melocotones
Peaches

Melones
Melons

Fresas (y helado de fresas)
Strawberries (and strawberry ice cream)

Albaricoques (particularmente el yogur de albaricoque)
Apricots (particularly apricot yogurt)

Ciruelas
Plums

Manzanas
Apples

Me gustan todas las frutas
—menos los limones.
I like eating all fruits—except lemons.

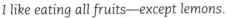

Me gusta el pan, con mucha mantequilla y mermelada.
I like bread, with lots of butter and jam.

Me gustan los bizcochos y las tortas.
I like cakes and tarts.

No me gustan mucho los huevos.
I do not like eggs much.
Me gusta mucho la carne, especialmente las hamburguesas.
I love meat, especially hamburgers.

 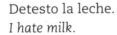

Me gusta beber Coca-Cola o té.
I like drinking Coca-Cola or tea.
Detesto la leche.
I hate milk.

Mi plato favorito son los spaghetti con salsa de tomate, queso y una salchicha.
My favorite dish is spaghetti with tomato sauce, cheese and a sausage.

En la escalera mecánica

Jerónimo, el gitano
Jeremy, the gypsy
¿Qué tiene debajo del brazo?
What does he have under his arm?

Miguel mira los anuncios.
Mike is looking at the advertisements.
En un anuncio ve una cama muy grande.
He sees a picture of a big bed.
Miguel no tiene cama.
Mike has no bed.

Alberto no le gusta la escalera mecánica.
Albert does not like the escalator.

Mauricio no necesita escaleras.
Maurice doesn't need a staircase.
Vuela por encima de todos.
He flies above everybody.

Un abrigo de piel
A fur coat

Un paraguas
An umbrella

Un bolso de compras
A shopping bag

Esta mujer está muy sorprendida de ver un loro.
This woman is very surprised to see a parrot.

On the escalator

Juan trata de bajar por la escalera que sube.
John is trying to go down the up staircase.

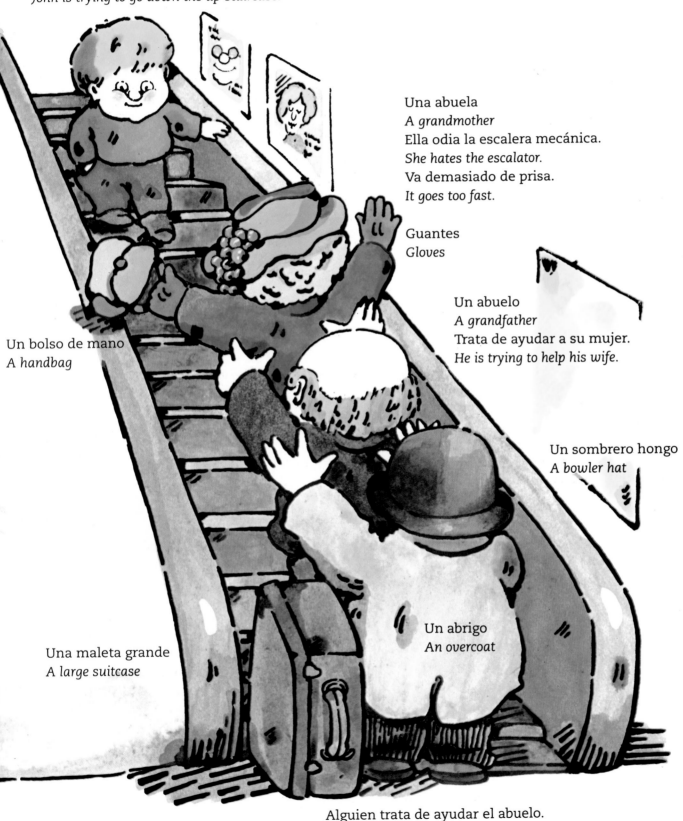

Una abuela
A grandmother
Ella odia la escalera mecánica.
She hates the escalator.
Va demasiado de prisa.
It goes too fast.

Guantes
Gloves

Un abuelo
A grandfather
Trata de ayudar a su mujer.
He is trying to help his wife.

Un bolso de mano
A handbag

Un sombrero hongo
A bowler hat

Una maleta grande
A large suitcase

Un abrigo
An overcoat

Alguien trata de ayudar el abuelo.
Somebody is trying to help the grandfather.

Jerónimo va a las carreras
Jeremy goes to the races

Jerónimo tiene hambre y frío.
Jeremy is hungry and cold.

Quiere comprar una manta y un poco
de queso.
*He wants to buy himself a blanket and some
cheese.*

Pero no tiene dinero.
But he has no money.

Pero tiene muchos brezos.
But he has a lot of heather.
Los trenza en pequeños ramilletes.
He makes it into lots of small sprigs.

Va a las carreras.
He goes to the races.
En el hipódromo hay mucha gente.
At the track there are lots of people.

Jerónimo vende algunos ramilletes de brezos.
Jeremy sells a few sprigs of heather.
La gente cree que el brezo trae suerte.
People think that heather is lucky.

Un gordo compra cuatro ramilletes.
A fat man buys four sprigs.

Su caballo va a correr en la próxima carrera.
His horse is going to run in the next race.
Necesita buena suerte.
He needs good luck.

De pronto, el gordo regresa.
Suddenly, the fat man comes back.
¡Su caballo ha ganado!
His horse has won!

El gordo está muy feliz.
The fat man is very happy.
Compra todos los brezos de Jerónimo.
He buys all Jeremy's heather.

Pero en dos horas Jerónimo sólo ha vendido
diez ramilletes.
*But in two hours Jeremy has sold only
ten sprigs.*

Jerónimo también está feliz.
Jeremy is very happy too.

¡Tiene bastante dinero para comprarse dos
mantas, queso, una caja de chocolates y un puro!
*He has enough money to buy himself two blankets,
some cheese, a box of chocolates and a cigar!*

Mi familia
My family

Uno de mis primos mayores
One of my big cousins
Se llama Pablo.
He is called Paul.
Es marinero.
He is a sailor.

Una de mis tías
One of my aunts
Un conejillo de Indias
acaba de morderla.
*A guinea pig has
just bitten her.*

Mi padre
My father
Su camisa es demasiado
estrecha.
His shirt is too tight.
Mi abuelo
My grandfather

Mi abuela
My grandmother
Tiene el pelo azul.
She has blue hair.

Mi
Me

Cuatro primos pequeños
Four little cousins

Mi tío
My uncle
Es hermano de mi padre.
He is my father's brother.
Son gemelos.
They are twins.

Otro tío
Another uncle
Es el marido de mi
tía favorita.
*He is my favorite
aunt's husband.*

Mi hermana
My sister
Le gusta mucho maquillarse.
She loves making herself up.

Mi padrino
My godfather

Mi tía favorita
My favorite aunt

Mi hermano
My brother

Mi madre
My mother
Está tratando de sonreír.
She is trying to smile.

Claudio es el perro de mi padrino.
Claude is my godfather's dog.

Tiene nueve años y tres conejillos de Indias.
He is nine, and he has three guinea pigs.

Casa en venta
House for sale

Esta casa está en venta.
This house is for sale.
La gente la está mirando.
People are looking at it.
¿Está terminada?
Is the house finished?

El cuarto de baño
The bathroom
¿Dónde está la bañera?
Where is the bathtub?

La cocina
The kitchen

La nevera
The refrigerator

76

Un dormitorio
A bedroom

¿Cuántas camas hay?
How many beds are there?

El comedor
The dining-room

La escalera
The staircase

Los albañiles y los pintores tienen hambre.
The builders and painters are hungry.

El vestíbulo
The hall

El salón
The living-room

Una silla
A chair

Un sofá
A sofa

Un sillón
An armchair

El jardín
The garden

Una niveladora
A bulldozer

Cristóbal Caballero admira a Pedro.
Christopher Caballero admires Peter.
El también quiere ser astronauta.
He too wants to be an astronaut.

Pedro está mirando su torta de cumpleaños.
Peter is looking at his birthday cake.

La Sra. de Molinero
Mrs. de Molinero
Ella hizo la torta ayer.
She made the cake yesterday.
Está muy orgullosa de ella.
She is very proud of it.

Bujías
Candles

La torta de cumpleaños de Pedro
Peter's birthday cake
Tiene forma de Luna.
It is in the shape of the moon.

Limonada
Lemonade

Un vaso
A glass

Bocadillos de tomate
Tomato sandwiches

Una taza
A cup

El mantel
The tablecloth

Un cuchill
A knife

¿Quién está debajo de la mesa?
Who is under the table?

e Pedro el astronauta
stronaut's birthday

La Sra. de Blanco
Mrs. de Blanco
Cuando Pedro vuelve de la Luna
siempre le recoje en su taxi.
*When Peter comes back from the moon
she always picks him up in
her taxi.*

A Miguel le encantan los cumpleaños.
Mike loves birthdays.
En particular le gustan
los cacahuetes.
*He particularly loves
peanuts.*

Cacahuetes
Peanuts

Una cuchara
A spoon

Helado de fresa
Strawberry ice-cream
Cristóbal Caballero ha traído dos grandes cubos de helado.
Christopher Caballero brought two large bowls of ice-cream.

Bocadillos de jamón
Ham sandwiches

Una corbata
A tie
Es un regalo del Profesor Julián.
It's a present from Professor Julian.
¿Cuántas estrellas puedes ver?
How many stars can you see?

Grandes edificios
Big buildings

Una fábrica
A factory
Todo el mundo trabaja.
Everybody is working.

Una escuela
A school
Casi todos trabajan.
Nearly everyone is working.

Un edificio de oficinas
An office building

Un edificio de apartamentos
An apartment building
¿Qué diferencias hay entre este
edificio y el de oficinas?
*What differences are there between this
building and the office building?*

Una biblioteca
A library
Hay libros por todas partes.
There are books everywhere.

Una catedral
A cathedral
Es muy antigua.
It is very old.

Un gran almacén
A department store
En este almacén puedes comprar todo lo que quieras.
In this store you can buy everything you want.

Gaviotas
Seagulls

Está lloviendo
It is raining.

Nubes
Clouds

Juan está mirando por la ventana.
John is looking out of the window.
Le gusta mucho el movimiento del aliscafo.
He loves the movement of the hovercraft.
Se siente feliz.
He is very happy.

La azafata
The flight attendant
Ella prefiere viajar en avió
She prefers traveling by pla

El agua del mar está salada.
The sea-water is salty.

Olas
Waves

Miguel en un aliscafo
Mike in a hovercraft

El capitán del aliscafo
The captain of the hovercraft.

Miguel está mirando por la ventana.
Mike is looking out of the window.
¿De qué color tiene la cara?
What color is Mike's face?
Se siente mareado.
He is feeling seasick.

Fidel también se siente mareado.
Fido is feeling sea-sick too.

Un pez
A fish

¿Cuántos peces puedes ver?
How many fish can you see?

El aliscafo
The hovercraft
No toca el agua.
It does not touch the water.
Flota sobre un cojín de aire.
It is on a cushion of air.

Los ladrones
The burglars

Es invierno.
It's winter.
Miguel y Fidel buscan un sitio caliente
donde pasar la noche.
*Mike and Fido are looking for a warm place
to spend the night.*

En la calle hay también dos ladrones.
In the street there are also two burglars.
Los ladrones van a la casa de los
Sres. de Blanco.
*The burglars go to Mr. and Mrs. de
Blanco's house.*

Rompen da cerradura de la puerta.
They break the lock on the door.
Los ladrones llenan sus sacos.
The burglars fill their sacks.

De pronto oyen un ruido.
Suddenly they hear a noise.
Juana de Blanco es sonámbula.
Jane de Blanco is walking in her sleep.

El Sr. y la Sra. de Blanco se despiertan.
Mr. and Mrs. de Blanco wake up.
El Sr. de Blanco telefonea a la policía.
Mr. de Blanco telephones the police.

Ellos creen que es un fantasma.
They think she is a ghost.
Huyen.
They run away.

El policía se lleva a los ladrones.
The police officer takes the burglars away.
El Sr. y la Sra. de Blanco dan gracias a Miguel.
Mr. and Mrs. de Blanco thank Mike.

Miguel y Fidel llegan.
Mike and Fido are there.
Están tratando de calentarse.
They are trying to get warm.
Miguel coje a los ladrones y Fidel ladra.
Mike grabs the burglars and Fido barks.

Le dan una cama caliente y confortable.
They give him a warm and comfortable bed.
Miguel y Fidel están muy felices.
Mike and Fido are very happy.

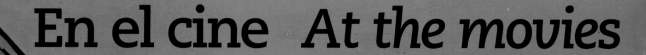

En el cine   *At the movies*

Los vaqueros llevan sombreros blancos.
The cowboys wear white hats.
Los pistoleros llevan sombreros negros.
The gangsters wear black hats.

Un telón de terciopelo rojo
A red velvet curtain

Una acomodadora
An usherette
Es una amiga de Silvia.
She is a friend of Sylvia's.

Ella vende chocolate y nueces.
She is selling chocolate and nuts.
¿Qué más vende?
What else is she selling?

Los espectadores
The audience

La Sra. de Moreno
Mrs. de Moreno
Ella odia las películas de vaqueros.
She hates westerns.
Tiene miedo a los pistoleros.
She is afraid of the gangsters.

El Sr. Moreno y María
Mr. Moreno and Mary
A ellos les gustan mucho las
películas de vaqueros.
They love westerns.

86

Miguel entra.
Mike is coming in.
Le gusta mucho ver películas.
He loves watching films.

Mauricio, Alberto y Fidel
Maurice, Albert and Fido
A ellos les gustan mucho
las películas de vaqueros.
They love westerns.
Pero no se les permite entrar en el cine.
But they can't go into the movies.

SALIDA
EXIT

Un reloj
A clock

LAVABOS
TOILETS

Silvia saca los billetes.
Sylvia takes the tickets.

Una pila eléctrica
A flashlight

Juan
John
Quiere ser vaquero.
He wants to be a cowboy.

¿Cómo viajan?
How do they get around?

El piloto vuela en un avión a reacción.
The pilot flies in a jet plane.

Jerónimo viaja en su casa rodante.
Jeremy gets around in his wagon.
Su caballo va muy despacio.
His horse goes very slowly.
Cuando el caballo tiene hambre, se para.
When he's hungry, the horse stops.

Fidel anda.
Fido walks.
Cuando está muy cansado, Miguel lo lleva en brazos.
When he is very tired Mike carries him.

Pedro viaja en una nave espacial.
Peter gets around in a spacecraft.

Mauricio vuela.
Maurice flies.
Va muy de prisa.
He goes very fast.
Nunca tiene problemas con el tráfico.
He never has problems with the traffic.

Miguel anda a pie.
Mike gets around on foot.
No anda muy de prisa.
He doesn't go very quickly.

La Sra. de Blanco viaja en su taxi.
Mrs. de Blanco gets around in her taxi.
Le gusta ir de prisa.
She likes going fast.
Cuando el tráfico está malo se pone furiosa.
When the traffic is bad she is furious.

El conductor de autobús viaja en un autobús
The bus driver gets around in a bus.

El millonario viaja en un gran yate.
The millionaire gets around in a big yacht.

A la Srta. Colina no le gusta ir de prisa.
Miss Colina doesn't like going fast.
Viaja en bicicleta.
She gets around on a bicycle.

María Moreno tiene patines.
Mary Moreno has got some roller skates.
A sus ratones blancos les gusta ir de prisa.
Her white mice love going fast.

¿Y tú?
And you?

¿Cómo viajas?
How do you get around?

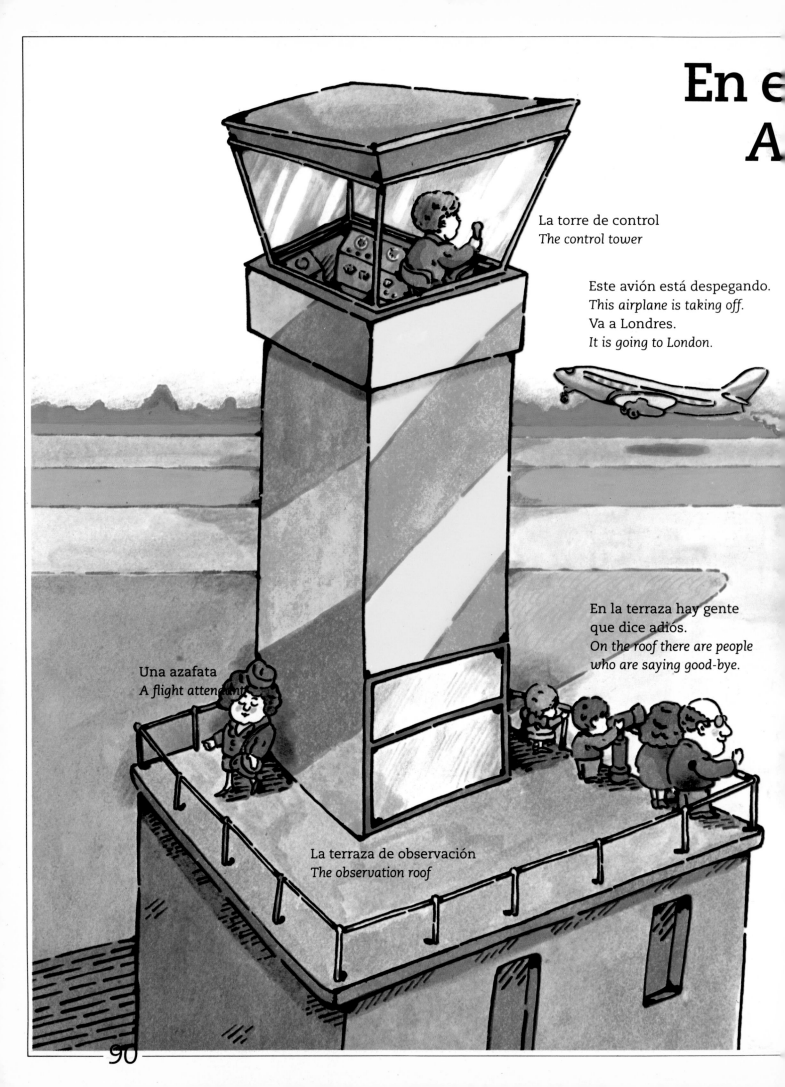

La torre de control
The control tower

Este avión está despegando.
This airplane is taking off.
Va a Londres.
It is going to London.

En la terraza hay gente
que dice adiós.
*On the roof there are people
who are saying good-bye.*

Una azafata
A flight attendant

La terraza de observación
The observation roof

Este avión está aterrizando.
This airplane is landing.
Uno de sus motores se ha averiado.
One of its engines has broken down.

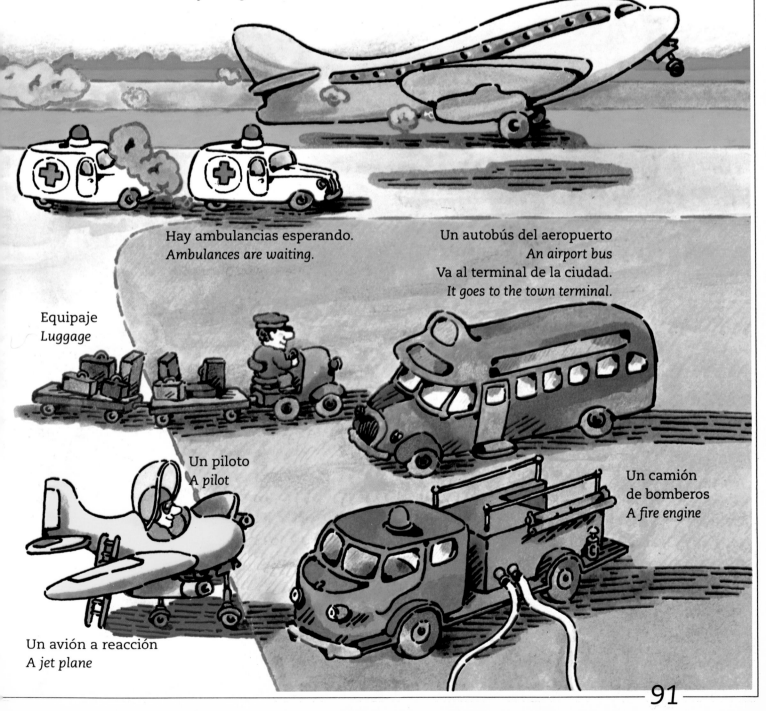

Hay ambulancias esperando.
Ambulances are waiting.

Un autobús del aeropuerto
An airport bus
Va al terminal de la ciudad.
It goes to the town terminal.

Equipaje
Luggage

Un piloto
A pilot

Un camión
de bomberos
A fire engine

Un avión a reacción
A jet plane

La Sra. de Molinero y Miguel hacen pan
Mrs. de Molinero and Mike make bread

La Sra. de Molinero y Miguel hacen pan.
Mrs. de Molinero and Mike are making bread.
Mezclan harina, agua y sal.
They mix together flour, water and salt.

Miguel trata de leer la receta.
Mike tries to read the recipe.

La Sra. de Molinero pone dos cucharadas de levadura.
Mrs. de Molinero puts in two spoonfuls of yeast.

Ponen el pan sobre el radiador.
They put the bread on the radiator.

El pan va a doblar de tamaño.
The bread will become twice as big.

La Sra. de Molinero y Miguel salen de la cocina.
Mrs. de Molinero and Mike go out of the kitchen.
El pan comienza a hincharse.
The bread begins to get bigger.

Una hora más tarde la Sra. de Molinero y Miguel regresan.
An hour later Mrs. de Molinero and Mike come back.

¡El pan se ha desbordado!
The bread has overflowed!
El radiador está cubierto de pan.
The radiator is covered in bread.

La Sra. de Molinero mira la receta.
Mrs. de Molinero looks at the recipe.

Había demasiada levadura en el pan.
There was too much yeast in the bread.

Es culpa de Miguel.
It's Mike fault.

La Sra. de Molinero toma un pedacito de pan.
Mrs. de Molinero takes a bit of the bread.
Lo come.
She eats it.

El pan está cocido.
The bread is cooked.
Todo está bien si acaba bien.
All's well that ends well.

Miguel y la Sra. de Molinero tienen
una cena deliciosa.
*Mike and Mrs. de Molinero have
a delicious supper.*

No se sientan a la mesa.
They don't sit at the table.

¡Comen del radiador!
They eat off the radiator!

¿Sabes?
Do you know?

Los meses del año
The months of the year

enero	*January*
febrero	*February*
marzo	*March*
abril	*April*
mayo	*May*
junio	*June*
julio	*July*
agosto	*August*
septiembre	*September*
octubre	*October*
noviembre	*November*
diciembre	*December*

Las estaciones del año
The seasons of the year

primavera	*spring*
verano	*summer*
otoño	*autumn*
invierno	*winter*

Los días de la semana
The days of the week

lunes	*Monday*
martes	*Tuesday*
miercoles	*Wednesday*
jueves	*Thursday*
viernes	*Friday*
sábado	*Saturday*
domingo	*Sunday*

La brújula
The compass

norte	*North*
sur	*South*
este	*East*
oeste	*West*

Viajando
Traveling

la carreterra	*the road*
la carreterra principal	*the main road*
la autopista	*the highway*
cerrada al tráfico	*closed to traffic*
se prohibe aparcar	*no parking*
camiones	*trucks*
sigan a la derecha	*keep right*
¡circulen!	*move along!*
¡cuidado!	*look out!*
una multa	*a parking ticket*
un policía	*a police officer*
¡socorro!	*help!*
lo siento	*I am sorry*
perdón	*excuse me*

Los continentes
The continents

Africa	*Africa*
Antarctica	*Antarctica*
Asia	*Asia*
Australia	*Australia*
Europa	*Europe*
América del Norte	*North America*
América del Sur	*South America*

Algunos países	Some countries
Argentina	Argentina
Australia	Australia
Austria	Austria
Bélgica	Belgium
Bolivia	Bolivia
Canadá	Canada
Islas del Canal	The Channel Islands
Chile	Chile
Colombia	Colombia
Dinamarca	Denmark
Ecuador	Ecuador
Inglaterra	England
Irlanda	Ireland
Finlandia	Finland
Francia	France
Alemania	Germany
Grecia	Greece
Holanda	Holland
Hungría	Hungary
Italia	Italy
Luxemburgo	Luxemburg
Méjico	Mexico
Nueva Zelanda	New Zealand
Irlanda del Norte	Northern Ireland
Noruega	Norway
Paraguay	Paraguay
Peru	Peru
Polonia	Poland
Portugal	Portugal
Rusia	Russia
Escocia	Scotland
Africa del Sur	South Africa
España	Spain
Suecia	Sweden
Suiza	Switzerland
Turquía	Turkey
Estados Unidos de América	United States of America
Uruguay	Uruguay
Venezuela	Venezuela
Gales	Wales

Algunos colores	Some colors
rojo	red
azul	blue
verde	green
amarillo	yellow
blanco	white
negro	black
violeta	violet
pardo	brown
rosa	pink
naranja	orange
castaño	maroon

Algunos números	Some numbers
uno	one
dos	two
tres	three
cuatro	four
cinco	five
seis	six
siete	seven
ocho	eight
nueve	nine
diez	ten
once	eleven
doce	twelve
trece	thirteen
catorce	fourteen
quince	fifteen
dieciséis	sixteen
diecisiete	seventeen
dieciocho	eighteen
diecinueve	nineteen
veinte	twenty
ciento	one hundred

A page for parents

I Can Read Spanish is not intended to be a child's only source of Spanish, but to be a supplement to other sources. For the child who knows no Spanish it can be used in English, with occasional Spanish words and phrases brought in as and when the parent feels the child can deal with them. In this way, the book can be used as a very gradual introduction to Spanish. However, it will probably be more widely used by children who know a little Spanish; and the following suggestions are given for such a child.

First of all, either the child reading the book, or the parent or friend, should know how to pronounce the Spanish words in it. To get the greatest benefit the child should read the words aloud, and whenever necessary should be helped with pronunciation (see **Reading Spanish**). Many of the words reappear several times in the book, and if they are pronounced wrongly the first time, will be thoroughly but incorrectly learned by the end of the book.

The section **Los amigos de Miguel** should be read first, as it introduces many characters who reappear throughout the book. After that, the sections can be read in any order as each is complete in itself. Children who know only very little Spanish should start with the sections which have the smallest number of sentences, for example **Desde el helicóptero** (page 26) and **De mañana en el jardin** (page 42). Usually the sections in full color contain a greater number of isolated words than the sections in two colors, many of which use sentences to tell a story.

After reading a few sections with both the Spanish and the English visible, many children will enjoy going back to one section and testing their knowledge by covering up the English with a piece of paper, and seeing how much of the Spanish they really know. The illustrations will help to show the meaning. The child should always study them when trying to find a meaning, rather than automatically refer to the English translation. If readers work out the meaning for themselves, and use the translation only as a final check, they are far more likely to remember what they have learned.

Throughout the book, occasional questions are asked, to which the reader should be encouraged to give answers in Spanish.

Its author hopes that *I Can Read Spanish* will entertain and teach at one and the same time.